Climbing Mountains
In The Dark

Cate Jacobs xx.

Climbing Mountains
In The Dark

Cate Jacobs

HEADLAND

First published in 2009
by
HEADLAND PUBLICATIONS
38 York Avenue
West Kirby, Wirral
CH48 3JF

Copyright © 2009 Cate Jacobs

British Library Cataloguing in Publication Data.
A full CIP record for this book is available from the British Library
ISBN
978-1-902096-52-0

Printed in Great Britain by
Oriel Studios, Orrell Mount
Hawthorne Road
Merseyside L20 6NS

To Molly, for the hope of all my tomorrows

CONTENTS

Part I

Part II

Part I

The Key To Your Heart

They told you - that under
the circumstances - your sex
life was over. A relationship
  - unlikely, to be careful who
you told, not to expect love.

I came along with neither
appointment nor invitation,
put my finger in the dip
at the bottom of your throat
and found that it fitted
like a key. I opened you
and discovered your heart
cowering in your ribcage
held to ransom by a HIV.

True Love

True love; is the sting of cystitis
and the dull ache of my pelvic bone
where I thought you'd wear me away,

It's the bruises of sleeplessness
- passionate insomnia that yawns
through the thirsty day after.

The wearing of your five o'clock
shadow in the rash on my face
(and my thighs), that peels like sunburn.

Watching dawn break together; anaemic
sunlight filtering through closed curtains,
sifting out the day, whilst we snuggle

down in each other's arms of craving.
And my eyes, smeared with yesterday's
mascara, could never see enough of you.

True love is being too happy to eat
and burning your mouth when you do.

Lawful Wedded Wife

I married you when you weren't looking
I snook behind your eyelids and whispered
I do.

Before You Loved Me

substitute love came
in the form
of prostitutes, porn,

a girl who gave you
scabies, and guilt
that engulfed you
like a sea of porridge;

a lover you had
nothing in common
with but desperation
and the safety of sex
with a woman
in the same situation;

before you loved me
with too much guilt
and desperation.

A Night to Remember

We had sausage, beans and mash for tea.
The children cleared the table, washed
the dishes and argued over who's turn it was
to dry. You had a cup of tea and a fag
by the open window. I wished for the wide
wings of an owl to fly out into the night with.

I ran the children a bath, swished up mountains
of bubbles that foamed over the side,
they lathered bubble beards and shaved
them off with stiff razor fingers, played
at being crocodiles and pirates. I wished
for a mermaids tail to swim down
the plughole and away to sea with.

I tucked them into bed, read them a story
of enchanted forests, unicorns, heroes
and kings, tussled their hair, kissed them,
goodnight - don't let the bed bugs bite
lingered to draw in their separate smells
wishing for a knight in shining armour
to whisk me away from tomorrow.

I picked up dirty clothes, put t-shirts
and grubby socks in the wash basket,
the lid back on the toothpaste, the tooth
brushes back in the jar; caught sight
of a misty me reflected in the bathroom
mirror - a fading apparition watching
from her looking glass world. As I hung
damp towels over the banister rail, I wished
I was Alice and could tumble away
down the rabbit hole.

Downstairs you watched the telly
with your feet up and smoked another
cigarette, whilst I sat on the edge
of the bed cradling the blood test bruise
in the curve of my arm, waiting for you
to come to bed; wishing I had pricked
my finger on a spindle, could sleep
away a hundred years and be woken
by a handsome prince with a cure.

D Day

It was a grey, wet day in June, when you stopped touching me.
I wondered if it was the rain drops in my hair that put you off
or the soil beneath my fingernails, or the dirt between my toes
or was it that I reminded you of an ink blot on a fresh page; spoiled,

tainted like a sheet of water-damaged, crumpled cotton, that never
quite comes clean again? Was it the dusty taste of death on my tongue
that repulsed you most, or my insistence that we speak now and no
it wouldn't wait for your wanting of a cup of tea and a fag first. I'd waited

all day, in the garden, turning the soil over in the rain, rehearsing the ground
of telling, pruning my words, weeding my tears. Looking for the ripe words
to tell you; we had reaped an unwelcome harvest, from one split second
of latexed love. A Christmas gift; not a Messiah, but this;

your worst nightmare,
                              wrapped in tissue paper.
                                             We said nothing

until a wet Friday in June when I sat at your feet and took your clean
hands in mine. My words changes our world forever, like the flood waters
of the monsoon rain drowning Noah; no rescue boat could save us now.
As two by two left one alone in stagnant silence. And you stopped
touching me.

HIV Haiku

How did you get it?
I was careless - it's corny
but I fell in love!

It

It fell between us
- fragile as fine blown glass -
and shattered our lives.

We walked barefoot
across the scattered fragments
until our feet bled;

millstones, grinding
love and experience
into deserts of sharp sand,

eating flesh from bone.
By breakfast time we sat
two skeletons at the table -

hourglass sand running
through our fingers -
waiting for eggs to boil.

Climbing Mountains in the Dark

we didn't hold hands,
we needed them
to steady ourselves
- wary of the ice
glistening
in the moonlight
that shone through
the branches
of winter trees.

fraught laugher
carried us upwards
to the summit
of orrest head
- where jolly
strangers
with flasks
of brandy,
bottles
of champagne
overindulgent
smiles and fireworks,
waited for midnight
- below us,
lake windermere,
opaque and blank
as the pupils
of your eyes -

we didn't hold hands
and you forgot to kiss me
when the clock struck twelve;
i was on your blind side
slipping on black ice.

Burning the Candle at Both Ends

We lit tallow candles

- attracting moths
with ragged wings,

that dip and weave
too close to the flame

leaving trails
of singéd obsession
behind, their tails on fire -

We lit tallow candles

knowing that all the melted
wax from Icarus' wings
couldn't put us back together again.

Crossing the Line

They confirmed
everything
in short hand;
HIV, CMV, AIDS.
As if there wasn't time
to say;
Human Immunodeficiency Virus
Cytomegalovirus
Acquired Immune Deficiency Syndrome

or sorry.

How long?

How
long
is
a
piece
of
string,
a
life,
my
hair,
his
inside
leg,
a
Singapore
sling,
the
time
we
have
left,
the
night
of
the
dead?

Secrets

Our secrets were silent
but never still, they shimmered,
a cold haze, hanging in the gaps
between us. Sat uninvited

at the tea table; interrupting
the conversation, dropping hints
on the floor, spilling onto the tablecloth
leaving invisible stains and contaminating

the children with their - not quite lies.
We turned the music up loud
- they screamed in the spaces
between one note and the next -

until we grew deaf and could
no longer hear each other.
They told bedtime stories
of monsters and dragons -

that jealously guard hoards
of truth in deep underground
caverns - who burn the fingers
and cut out the tongues, of those

who ask too many questions.
They crept into the sandman's sack,
cast with sleep into the corners
of your eyes and blinded you.

The Book of Goodbyes

You read borrowed books
from the library (one of few
places we still went together -
the library and the hospital)
as if you were searching
for; answers, an explanation, the story
of your life, a happily ever after.

You read. Always hungry
for more; growing thinner.

My mother gave you a copy
of *'A Suitable Boy'*
you joked as to whether you had been,
on reflection, a suitable boy, for her daughter,
wondered if you'd live long enough
to get to the end of it.

You read slowly, deliberately,
as if every page mattered
or measured out the days left
to live in beautiful phrases.
When you reached the end

you took your library card
and left me;
went home to your mother.

The Last Waltz

His guilt grew like bindweed
tendrils wrapped themselves
around my unsuspecting ankles.
I thought they were bracelets,
white bridal bells pealing celebration
but they crept up my legs
and stopped me from dancing.

He unlaced the ribbons from my
shoes, wound them up carefully,
put them away in an old biscuit
tin, amongst twists of baby wool,
odd buttons, half used spools of cotton,
safety pins and dusty tailor's chalk,
before waltzing away...2 3...1 2 3...
1 2 3....without me.

Keys

You never said goodbye
you just came home one day
put your house keys on the table
asked me for the car key back
and drove away.

Sipping Peppermint Tea

He could have ordered
a cappuccino with cocoa dust
sprinkles melting into milky

froth or a latte in a tall glass
with a twisted napkin tied
around its neck like a kerchief.

He could have chosen
a mocha, an Americano,
a cold frappe, a hot chocolate

- a blob of whipped cream, floating
marsh mallows, chocolate flakes
and cinnamon, but no, he ordered

an espresso - two mouthfuls
of bitter blackness in a mean cup,
which he knocked back

like the last shot of life.

She turned away from him
sipping peppermint tea.

Disbanded Love

In the stillness of your absence,
flowers decay quietly;
graveyard bouquets
of lilies and geraniums.

The empty spaces
you left behind are filled
with an odd sock
a dried out toothbrush
rusty razor blades
an old sports supplement
a half eaten jar of piccalilli
4oz of liquorice pieces
an unopened bottle of tequila
a mountain bike with two flat tyres
and a box of cornflakes.

Sorry recompense
for spent love gone sour,

like the full cream milk
in the fridge I don't drink;
turning to cheese.

Coming to Your Senses

smell

Sometimes in the evening I wear your old jumper
against my bare skin, light one of your cigarettes -

let it burn until it's one long ash of cremated tobacco,
the room full of smoke - I iron your pyjamas hot,

put them on and crawl into bed, wondering if you
still swim in your dreams, whether you wake

with the feint fragrance of chlorine on your skin.

sound

There was always a neatly trimmed
line between the moustache of your

beard and your top lip, a thin white
road of shaven skin outlining your kiss.

When I walked into your dying room,
it was still there, a yellowing meniscus

of crinkled parchment, clutching the silence
of all the things you didn't say and now

it's too late, the words won't come;
stuck in your throat, they gargle and dribble

down your chin, refusing to be swallowed.

sight

If eyes are windows your curtains are drawn
in stagnant blue greens, like sea water in a jam jar
going murky in the sunlight. Once they were rock

pools where sirens swam and starfish
twinkled - now nothing shines
except for a droplet of the ocean
which I catch on my finger and drink.

touch

even your skin feels different -
like the skin on cooling custard
it wrinkles lukewarm to cold clammy.

taste

hello had high notes of cucumber,
bursting with lychee's and mango
edged with traces of baby's breath;

goodbye tastes of chicory, bitter
orange, rue and sorrel leaves
with undertones of sugared almonds.

Carrier

These arms have carried; tired
children home from school,
had coats and bags
dumped across them, leaving
me to lumber up the street
a pack horse, beast of burden
tied to pullovers, paintings, lunch
boxes, while the children ran free.

These arms have carried;
bags of shopping on the bus
when the housekeeping wouldn't
stretch to a taxi; buckets, spades
and picnics to the beach; pushed
lawn mowers across football pitch
lawns and dug over vegetable patches,
carried pans of soup and secrets to the table.

These arms have carried;
bundles of driftwood for the fire,
baskets of fruit, puzzle books, word
searches, bottles of lucozade - hospital
visit paraphernalia that never made you better.
These arms carried your coffin up the aisle
as The Verve sang *'the drugs don't work......'*

Your arms will never hold me again,
but they wait to carry me
over the threshhold of breath
- when the time comes -
you promised to be there.

Betrayal

I sat alone in a bath of tepid water

drinking
cranberry juice
hiding
amongst the bubble baths
and shampoos
weeping
hugging my knees
rocking
back and forth
hoping
that he would comfort me.

But he did not come,
then,
or any other day
or night
or dawn
or dusk
or Christmas
or birthday.
He never came.

So I painted the bathroom like the night sky
ran a deep hot bath,
dissolved a handful of dead sea salts
scattered rose petals on the water,
tucked my nakedness beneath the surface
and finally went to sleep.

Haircut

A number four, she said
Are you sure? he answered, letting
her hair spill through his fingers
like ribbons of water. *Do it.* she replied

He took the clippers in his hand,
adjusted the head and rested them
on her temple - *No turning back!*
- Nothing to turn back for.

Nothing to turn back for nothing
to live for either - a moment of perfect
balance - the clippers buzzed, vibrated,
hesitated against her hairline. Taking

a deep breath he swept them back and forth
until her scalp was soft bristled, and long
curls of auburn hair, covered the lino
like tongues of fire with no words

to name her sorrow or whisper comfort.
She gathered them together, held them up
like the tail of a slain fox, brushed it over
her cheek, paid the barber and left.

Scarification

I would have preferred a cattle brand
a searing mark, singed through soft layers
of skin, scorching through to the bone.
I would have welcomed the pain,
the scarred burned tissue of torture.
I would have picked at the scab,
rubbed it with salt, charcoal, the ashes
of you and let it bleed in dirty dribbles.

Instead in a sterile studio, the tattooist
snapped on a fresh pair of latex gloves,
wiped my arm with antiseptic, opened
a new needle and pricked designer ink
beneath my skin - an epitaph in Celtic blue.

Cold Feet

I scoured the house,
turned out cupboards
shook books by their spines,
 - certain there must be a message
a letter, something you
had forgotten to give me.

Something other
than silence and dust.

At the back of your empty drawer
I found a pair of Fair isle socks in green.
Are your feet cold without them?

Casual Grief

After you died
I fucked a lot.
Fucked for the affirmation
of life, of desirability,
of pretending to be normal.

Normal
raced away
without a backwards glance
and left me by the roadside
an untouchable
out of bounds kind of girl.
A casualty of fuck and run,
bandaged with numbness
sitting in the gutters of grief
pretending
that everyone who passed
nomadically through my bed,
loved me really.

But after sunset,
the cold space beside me
gnawing at my sleeplessness,
my heart would ache
across the darkness
longing to be warm again.

Daylight Savings

I opened an account
and began to deposit moments from days
I wanted to remember. Banked memories
accumulating interest for the rainy days
of forgetfulness and grey hair; of drawing
my pension and riding the bus for free.

I deposited:

the sunrise on an ice cold mountain
a cloud of frozen breath and the snow angels
we made side by side.
My father's voice reading me a bedtime story.
The day my first child was born,
the new smell of him warm and milky
like cinnamon and earth after rain
and you singing him happy birthday.

I would deposit

Good Friday and the endless baking of buns,
hot, cross and steamy, oozing butter drips
til teatime. And the middle of the day when no one
was home and I could be still, without you

and now that I am, I withdraw all the days
one by one and live them slowly backwards.

Anniversary

Another year turns
across the grief o'clock
of mourning that ticks
to the beat of my heart,
a sundial of shadows
hidden in the sorrow
of living without you.
In a sunless garden
of memories fading
with the receding light
of togetherness
picking snowdrops alone.
Renting time.

Cherry Tree Execution

When the new neighbours came
they erected a fence, to mark
the boundary line between

us and them.

They dug up the limestone dance floor
that hosted yesterdays garden parties,
chopped down the cherry tree and built

a car park.

The hurt space in the sky quivers
with the memory of cherry blossoms,
Two white butterflies flutter

like thin ghosts

around the severed stump -
now an amputated grave
marker for the scattered

ashes of friends.

A Question of Survival

survival 1.*the state or fact of surviving*
i survived - they died
why me?

2.*an object or practice that has survived from an earlier time*
object - me
practice - living
earlier time - before HIV
why not me?

natural selection.
did it select me because
i'm a natural sort of girl?
 - having it makes me
feel very unnatural.

thought:
sometimes survival
is the worst alternative there is.

Left Behind;

abandoned deserted forsaken
cast aside stranded rejected
dumped ditched disused
neglected idle unoccupied
uninhabited empty reckless
unrestrained wild unbridled
impulsive impetuous
immoderate, wanton.

I have been all of these.

I whisper the words - that hide
behind my teeth - into a match
box, leave it up the chimney
for Father Xmas. He's the one
who hears my confession

Forgive me Father for I have wished
for a normal life expectancy,
a cure, the resurrection of the dead,
to own my own home, see my children
grow up, graduate become a grand
mother and live and love
in a world where I belong
and red ribbons are what I tie
around my Xmas presents.

just below my skin
i'm screaming   *(Salva mea - Faithless)*

see me
i am more than this
the sum of a blood test
a collection of cells
or a virus,
i am human,
i am woman
i am warm
i am cold
i laugh,
i cry
i am sexy
i bleed,
i need.

I need for you
to see me not be me

i'm screaming…..
just below my skin.

Pass the Parcel

I wrapped my heart in sheets
of newspaper - cut the stars out
of my eyes and slipped them
between the layers with the forfeits

of love.

A cross legged circle of boys
wearing the masks of men, tossed
the parcel to each other like a rugby
ball, grabbing it out of the air when

the music stopped, clutching it
into the nest of their stomachs
and folded legs. Pressing it against
their stiffening groins, groaning,

squeezing it tight, falling forward
onto their knees, shredding the paper
- a confetti of hopes and false promises
torn away - revealing the prize.

I wrapped my heart in yesterday's news
3/4lb of dripping meat, tied it up
with bows of my hair, passed the parcel
to a circle of men with blood on their hands.

Part II

Attraction

Whirlwind blows a storm
Invisible alchemy
Turns my heart to you
I see you for the first time
But you don't know I'm here. Yet.

Falling

If I fell in love
with you, would you catch me -
or leave me falling?

Undertones

Beneath the aftershave
and scent of shampoo,
you smell like the wind
on limestone moors,

tinged with a hint of wild
sun beaten heather;
where deep lagoons
nestle in waiting,
between sentry rocks,
guarding the secret pathways
to places we have never swum.

Beyond the shallow sight
of eyes dimming, I see who
you are and love you with
no expectation of love in return.

Birthday Kiss

I should have been in Casablanca

wrapped in the warm trade winds
of Moroccan sunshine
with the dust of yesterday

sifting through my sandals
leaving grit between my toes
Instead I was here,

eating chips and drinking
sour beer on a long table
of friends in a basement bar.

Later when the birthday
drinks had run dry, leaving
sticky residues clinging

to the window of today,
we sat drinking tea
in the candlelight together.

Just you and I.

*

And the morning after

with headache in tow
I made a pot of coffee
drank ½ pint of orange juice

went back to bed and wondered
what the shape of you, curled
against me would feel like.

Waiting by the Telephone.

16.06
I sit by the river watching aeroplanes
taking people I don't know
to destinations from which they will
never send me postcards.

I sit beneath the four o'clock sun
in my bare feet, wishing
that the mobile in my shoe
would ring and that it was you.

Instead my skin burns
I forgot to wear protection.
A dragonfly hovers over the water.
The phone remains silent.
16.09

Fisherman

He baits his hook with cooked prawns
pink and curled in on themselves
waiting to be unfurled by the soft suck
of lips below the water.

He casts the line long, where the willow
bends low. Dips the tip of his rod, to rest
on ripples that the wind shatters, scattering
light in broken shards of mid afternoon green.

The rod quivers. The line tightens, cutting
the water like a cheese wire. He reels in.
Lets a little slack. Reels faster. It resists.
A head breaks the surface. He jerks the rod,

landing the fish on the bank. She looks up at him.
He takes her firmly in his cupped hands,
her tail flicks and twitches. Her open mouth
gulps air as he slides the hook out.

She lies still in his hands. Lubricating his skin
with water and salt slime. Scenting his fingers.
Later he will recall the cool curve of her body
her length, her weight, the colours of her scales,

the silent gasp she made as he held her,
the splash of her escape; and her name.

Shaggy Ink-cap
Coprinus comatus

In the morning you were there
a surprise on a grass pillow.
An overnight miracle rising
erect, cylindrical, pinkish and brown
over the bell-like end. Growing
from five to twelve centimetres.
You are delicious to eat, smeared
in butter, melting on my tongue

then gone, like a one-night stand,
before breakfast. You leave a pool
of black ink on green wet grass
- a dissolved telephone number.
Your rooting base deliquesces,
and you delicately drown in oxygen.

(*Deliquesce* – to dissolve slowly in water absorbed from the air.)

Here

Don't go, stay here,
where muscle and sinew speak
in the slip and slide
of perspiration,
in the wind and twist
of skin.

Here;

where clinging
is more than
insecurity
less than
desperation
as strong as the suck
of a limpet on hard rock
at low tide.

Where holding is;
the breath before release
and the wrap of arms
we rest in afterwards,
the measured squeeze of my yoni
dripping sea flavours
of love. Staining
the sheet beneath us.

And leaving is;
the peel of skins separating
the passing you the tissues
the time it takes to go
to the bathroom and back
the making of a cup of tea
the lighting of a cigarette
the getting dressed
and the closing of the door.

Don't go. Stay here.
Between my thighs,
where it's warm.

Neo Virgin

I shaved away my pubic hair.
My shame fell
I was naked,
hairless,
clean again.

Biopsy

(i)

There's a hole in my breast
a puncture wound leaking
a distilled consommé
of milk and motherhood.

(ii)

The clocks
are stuck ticking
ever forwards
and away.
Taking time.

(iii)

Poppies fade, petals fall
and we forget
- despite our best intentions.

Everything is pink now;
the snap dragons growing
for Saskia, the white rabbit's
eyes, candyfloss, strawberry
ice cream, the memory
of school blancmange
- when my chest
was a flat, tiny nippled,
plain of pink skin, soft
as a suckling pig.

Regimented lines of daffodils
are on parade, in fields of hope,
trumpeting the last post in yellow.

Premature Harvest

Bruised damsons weep
raw flesh, soft and bleeding.
Stay inside Saskia
it's not safe out here
the wasps are swarming.

Saskia

your name
is a whisper
a secret psalm
a prayer in pink
the yellow glow
of a buttercup held
beneath my chin.

In The Mud of Eden;

I am catching falling feathers
from a raven's wings.

Chanting prayers, weaving water
lilies and lotus flowers;

threading apple blossoms
and rosebuds into a crown

for you; twisting rowan twigs
and hawthorn, into wands.

In the mud of Eden;

I am imagining all the tiny
things that will make you pretty;

the slithers of your lips, the moons
on your fingernails, your toes,

your sea shell ears, the dip
of your chin, the lap of your tongue.

The north wind ripples
the grass, a tide of green,

swim Saskia, swim home
with the salmon.

In her fragile cradle, an amniotic
sea, rocks her gently. Hush hush

sleep now, I am singing
you lullabies in pink and lilac.

Wait Saskia, wait, while I sacrifice
a lamb to line your incubator.

Don't Spill the Sugar

The average baby weighs 6-8lbs
3-4 bags of sugar.
You weigh less than half a bag
full - a small scoop of sugar dust
- every grain counts.

Polarities of Breath

She climbs
new mountains, reaching
for the sky from incubated
dreams. She knows
no limits, only on and on.
No one tells her stop;
instead we sing, bake cakes
and buy her crampons,
for the frozen peaks
where the oxygen is thin
and still and blue.

She sleeps;
a translucent wisp of life
fragile and pink - a featherless
phoenix or a Snow White
waiting for her kiss into life.

You are born;
but not quite here yet,
little one, you came too soon.
Listen…daddy is whistling
for a wind to fill your sails
breathe Molly breathe.

Love Song in Base Ten

I love you
I love you two
I love you three
I love you four
I love you five
I love you six
I love you seven
I love you eight
I love you Nain
I love you

(* Nain - Welsh for grandmother)

Lifeline

Your hands overwhelm me
the palms of them too small
to hold a single kiss or a snowflake

You hold the future in those hands
it is written there, a tiny prophecy
mapped permanently in skin.

Shoes for Saskia

Her insteps arc wantonly
away from the earth;

wanting her to stay
I buy her electric blue

Wellington boots for all
the puddles we have yet

to splash in. You laugh
at me and say that she

could sail away to sea
in one of the boots -

being so small - afraid
that she might drown,

I sew a seal skin
into moccasins for Molly.

Mewing for Milk

The harvest moon hangs
in the night sky, full
and round and ripe.

The baby cries,
mewing for milk
and love and touch

and air to breathe.
Daddy whistled
- and the wind came;

a breath of time
on an unmapped course
of isobars. You turn

into the wind, figurehead
of your own ship,
mermaid child,

head above the wave
that sets you down
in your mothers arms.

She strokes your cheek,
washing over you, the spit
of love on her finger.

HIV Harpy

I am

a damned
death spirit,
with ripped
shadow

impenetrable
wings
and cold
blue kisses.

Beware

my lips
they seek

you.

CD4 Sunset

The sun dips over the edge
of the horizon. The end of a long
day cast in pinks, apricots,
deepening blues and purples -
bruising the sky with left overs
of light, acquiescing to the night.
Combinations of stars, like tablets
map an inevitable destiny.

Craving Rain

This weakness crept
upon me, like summer
rolling over and making
room for autumn amongst
sloe berries and the bones
of slaughtered lambs boiling
in the pot for soup.

When we left home
it was winter. Here on
this idyllic island of sun,
sea, sand and mountains,
paradise, is lost. Gritty

black sand rubs between
my toes - volcanic
leftovers, ground down
to itching powder that
sticks in delicate places
and chaffs under elastic.

The sun dries
my eyes, and I
find myself craving rain.

Washing the Beach Away

A high tide of HIV washes
through my veins,
like the undercurrent
at Valle Gren Ray

on spring equinox,
that steals the sand
from the beach
leaving only pebbles,

like fallen pills.

They say if I swallow
like a good girl
that one day the tide will wash
the beach back to me

Silent Sea

The ocean turns waves
the colour of your eyes
onto this pebbled beach -
 sea blue? sea green?

- we never could agree.
I sit, waiting for your
last words on the wind…
if there's ever anything

*you need…*the ocean
turns over waves
the colour of your eyes
and the sear and suck

of seawater over pebbles
says live…live…live.

Climbing Mountains in the Dark
(For Alison Hargreaves 1962 - 1995)

You died on August 13th 1995
- a cruel wind, whipped you off
Savage Mountain at a 100mph,

leaving only a legacy of footprints
- an autobiography written in snow,
a map to mummy's mountain.

At ground zero they questioned:
should mothers climb mountains?
I thread white ribbons and courage

through the eyelets of my boots,
in memory of you, and climb up
through the darkness and the laurel

forests. The night air grows cold.
I cough, with summit fever beading
on my forehead at 100 degrees.

Salted drops of fear and sweat drip
into my eyes and blind me. I am
with Paul on the road to Damascus

or is it the tower of Babel? God speaks
in a shower of rocks, we flatten ourselves
small and watch his wrath pass us by.

We are Adam and Eve, in the garden
of Eden, hiding the truth amongst the stars
of the zodiac, that heralds the death of us.

I know why the caged bird sings; its breast
pierced by an acacia thorn, spilling love
in a futile gesture of self sacrifice, the hope

of immortality tucked between its feathers,
expecting the freedom of release and wide skies.
K2 claimed you; HIV waits in the wings for me.

Communion

With a sharpened axe
in one hand and myne
in the other, he led me
into the wood, past ancient
oaks and groves of beech,

down the ley lines that lead
to the place where heaven
caresses
earth and the linden tree grows.

With one fell swoop
of his axe, the tree crashed
to the ground in a dust of lime
pollen. In white wood flesh he
gouged out the totem pole story
of us and nailed me to the cross-
bar of eagles wings, like Isis,

weeping bitter tears of tannin
 - the ink of wasted hope
that writes the history of love
in withered sentences. He turned
and walked away, leaving me
bleeding, in remembrance of him.

Photograph

Your face gazes
out from behind
a gauze of tissue
paper. A captured

moment in a day
we spent together
when you were
radiant and un-

self conscious
of my lens
which focused
to find your

beauty - held it
frozen in time -
iridescent siren
with a half smile

and a wisp of hair
kissing the corner
of your mouth.
You looked back

down my lens
in a bond of seeing,
an invisible link.
When I pressed

the shutter,
the moment
was severed,
like the umbilical

that once attached
us to each other.

txt msg's

Gud mornin me dear.
I sense yr pain deeply :(
u have a wise insight & yes
the layers r peeling away. He
is utterly cruel & basically rude.
I feel like shouting at him!!!!!
What about the temple 2moro? :)

Havin a bad day - my emotions
r rocking about. Feelin grief stricken
& on the edge. Spending money I ain't got
on the credit card - 8 pairs of lacy knickers, 3 bra's
& a pork chop was the latest spree! Can't stop crying.
I'm worn out with it all - have u got a fairy godmother
with a magic wand?

Wish I had. Grief takes time to dissipate u must
trust yrself yr doin well & things are only gonna get better.
Remember u r a strong intelligent beautiful woman who in time
will win thru. One final thought - a girl needs new knickers to start a new
life! Not sure how u will accessorize the pork chop though! C u 2moro x x x

Riddle

Silence lies between us
like a blanket
of smog, woven in wet wool.

I can not lift it and you do not try.

You sit and eat at my table
but never invite me for tea.
You sleep in my bed
I do not lie beside you.
Your candles burn on my altar
I do not pray there.
Your clothes hang in my wardrobe
I hang by a thread.

Who am I?

Jilted

Licking the taste of her
from his lips, he spits,
and walks away in fine rain,

the rusty taste of shame
tingling on his tongue.

Unfinished Tapestry

She unpicks
the frayed
and tattered edges
of morning,

unravelling the blue
and grey threads
of the sky
they once shared;

woven air,
which she
can no
longer breathe.

Threading
her needle
with the scent
of lilacs,

she darns
the hole
in the sky
and embroiders

a new day.

Happily Ever After

is a simple twist of fate
around the next bend
along the road to no where
across a desert chasing a horse
with no name. It's the heart
with no strings, the sky that never
rains, the moon that's always full
the cupboard that's never empty
a fish from the sea of plenty.
It's where time has already healed
the wounds yet to be inflicted
and love never dies
and it never ends in tears
here in the castle in the air
where we all live

happily ever after.

Drawing My Pension

When I am a pensioner, will they give me a box
of coloured pencils and paints to draw my pension with?

I'd like it to be purple on a Thursday in wintertime,
so that i can wrap it around myself like a warm cloak.

On a Tuesday in summer, I'd paint it yellow and green,
for egg and cress sandwiches and days at the beach.

On a Sunday in autumn I'd print it with leaves and take
it to listen to the brass band in the park with a flask of tea.

And once a year, on my birthday, I would paint myself
transparent and run around naked with new lambs.

And when I die, would you colour it for me, in bright
balloons of every colour that's left in the paint box?

Colour them across the sky, until the box is empty.

Acknowledgements

Some of these poems have appeared in *Poetry Pool 2 & 3* (Headland Publications) and *In the Red* magazine.

Thanks go to:

my Dad, for buying me a copy of *Amigo* when I was a little girl and instilling a love of poetry in me. Paul Foo (Llanishen High) for challenging me to write a poem, instead of giving me a detention. David Smith (Burnley High School for Girls!) for reading us *Summer with Monika,* and other gentle texts, when Chaucer got too heavy! Kaite O'Rielly, for helping me to believe I am indeed a poet and not just someone who writes poetry. Edmund Cusick for creating the Degree In Imaginative Writing at Liverpool John Moores University and filling our lives with magic and stories - and to the staff for their inspiring teaching! Martin and Paul, for mountains climbed and summits never conquered.

Special thanks go to:

The Hat Gang for fun, laughter, friendship, the iambic pentameter trot, honest feedback, ah Africa and organic moments! Alice Bennett for giving me a deadline! Bob Knowles for giving me a home and a table to write at when life got tough. My three fairy godmothers; Rebecca Dittman, Marian Sloan and Alison Stewart for IT support, cream cakes and gin! Jude McLoughlin for long walks by the sea and climbing mountains in the daylight with me. Tracey Mathias, fellow writer and friend for 40 years, also my many other friends and family, for on going love, encouragment and support. Particular thanks and honour to Elizabeth Welsh - the mother of my grand daughter.

And finally to my children, Bill, Tom and Rosanne Spencer, who have travelled, up hill and down dale, in the shadow of the mountain, with me. Yours was never an easy journey. You have been wonderful companions and a great example to others - in the early days of my HIV diagnosis, you gave me a reason to breathe and a desire to live - I could not have done this without you.